Flick the Switch!

Contents

Written by Clare Helen Welsh

Collins

What is electricity?

Electricity is a type of energy that powers devices that can be plugged in and switched on. Which of these items use electricity?

car

phone

pencil

apple

toothbrush

lamp

computer

2

Have you ever had a power cut in your home?

Fascinating fact

Most electrical items were invented less than 100 years ago.
Think what the world was like without electricity.

How is electricity produced?

Electricity is produced at power stations. It can be generated using renewable sources, like wind, and non-renewable sources like coal.

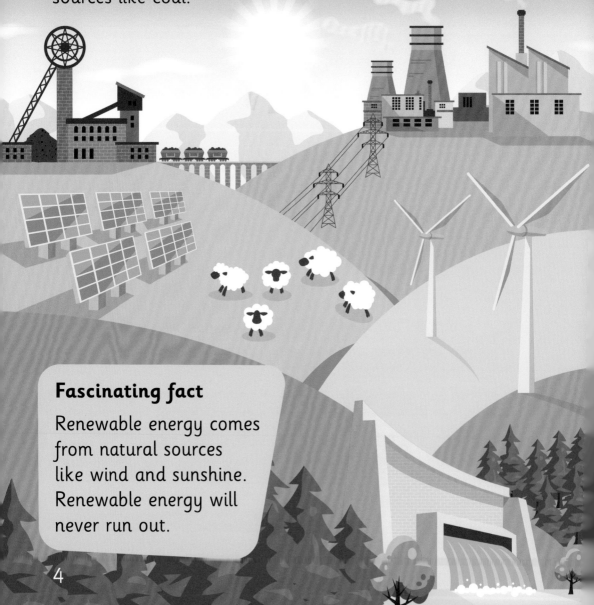

Fascinating fact

Renewable energy comes from natural sources like wind and sunshine. Renewable energy will never run out.

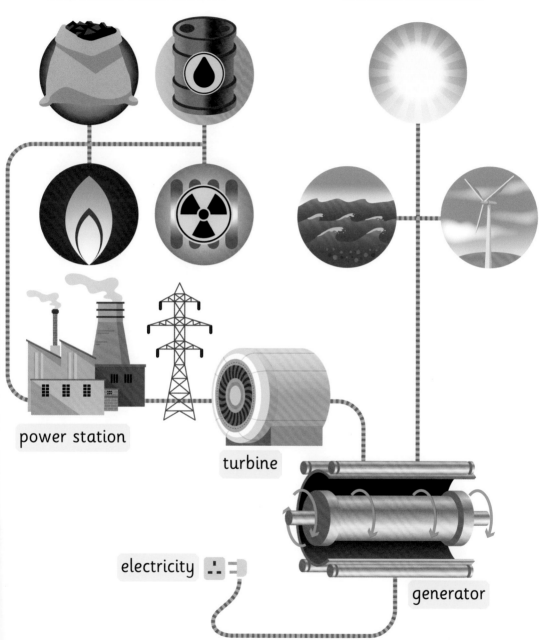

non-renewable sources

renewable sources

power station

turbine

electricity

generator

Distribution

Transmission lines transport electricity between power stations and pylons.

Pylons carry electricity over long distances.

Pylons connect to smaller power lines, which carry electricity to neighbourhoods.

Power lines run overhead and supply electricity to houses.

Electricity flows into the sockets and switches of our homes along the wiring.

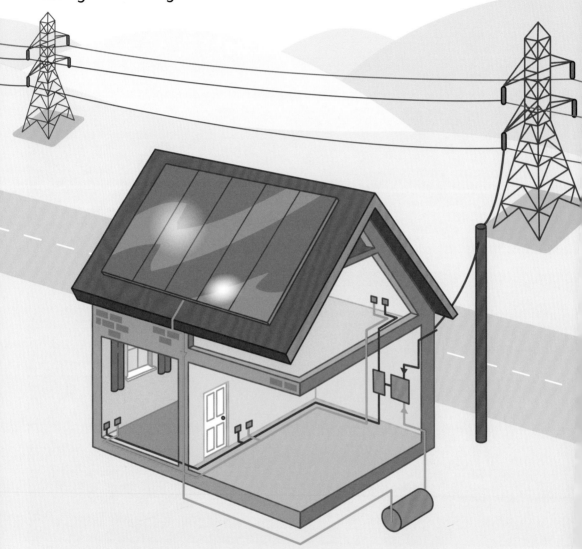

Wires are hidden beneath floors and walls.

A plug safely connects devices to mains electricity.

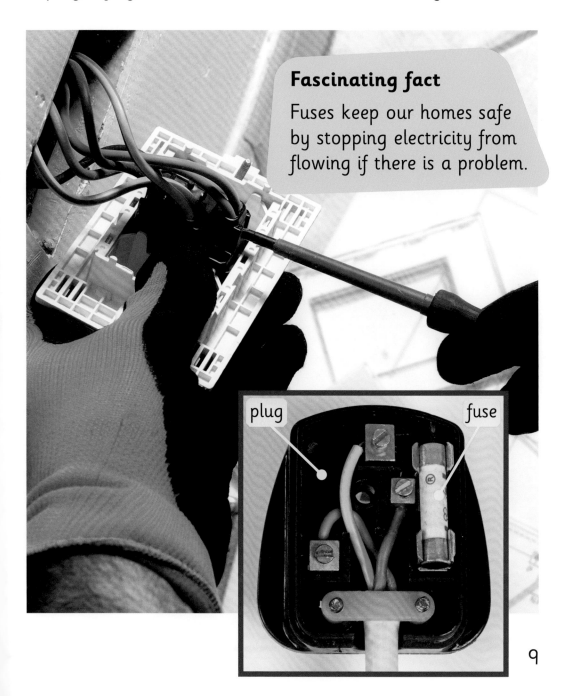

Fascinating fact

Fuses keep our homes safe by stopping electricity from flowing if there is a problem.

plug

fuse

9

How do batteries work?

Batteries contain special chemicals that combine and create electrical energy when they are switched on.

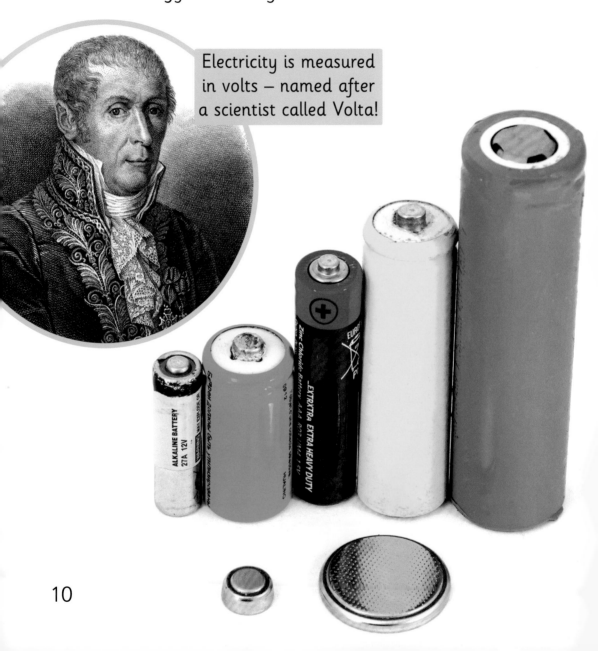

Electricity is measured in volts – named after a scientist called Volta!

10

You can turn potatoes into a battery by inserting nails and pieces of copper wire. Connecting the nails and wire will make the clock work without its battery!

copper wire

nail

potato

clock

Lightning

Electricity can be made by
humans or found naturally
on Earth. Ben Franklin
discovered that lightning and
electricity were the same thing.

Franklin designed the "lightning rod", which protects skyscrapers in storms by sending electricity safely to the ground.

Fascinating fact

One lightning bolt can power 100 lamps for a whole day!

Electric animals

Some eels and rays produce electric shocks for protection. Sharks use their snouts to detect electricity from prey that is far away or hiding.

shark

electric eel

electric ray

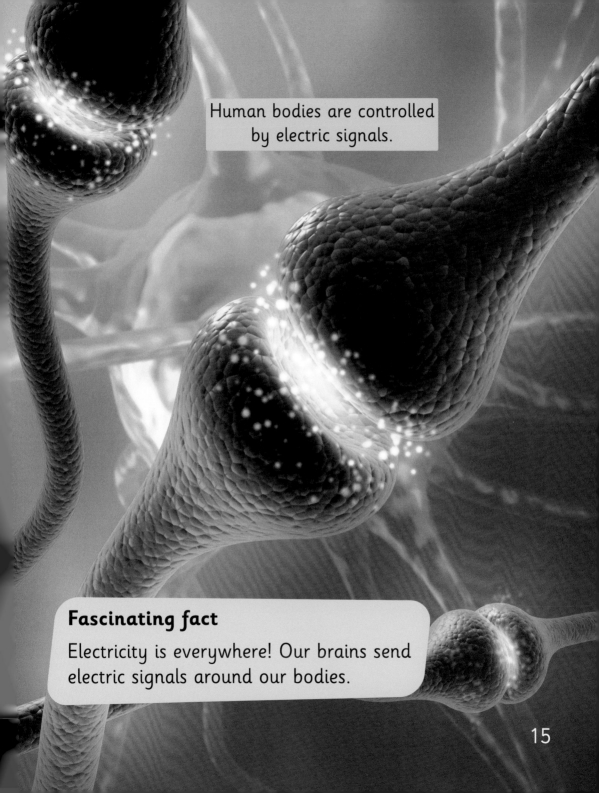

Human bodies are controlled by electric signals.

Fascinating fact

Electricity is everywhere! Our brains send electric signals around our bodies.

Static electricity

Electricity that isn't moving is static electricity. Some experts think geckos use static electricity to climb walls.

Try making static electricity by rubbing a balloon on your jumper.

Static electricity from the balloon can make your hair stand on end!

17

Staying safe

Electricians are specially trained to work with electricity.

Here are some precautions for being safe near electricity:

Don't ... play with sockets.

Don't ... fly kites near pylons.

Don't ... use electrical devices near water.

Don't ... climb trees near power lines.

Don't ... pull wires.

Saving electricity

Generating electricity from non-renewable sources is bad for the environment. It's important not to waste electricity and to reduce energy consumption where possible.

Energy-saving suggestions:

Turn off devices when not in use.

Car share, walk or cycle to school.

Shop locally to reduce the number of car trips you make.

Flick the switch

After reading

Letters and Sounds: Phases 5–6

Word count: 503

Focus phonemes: /n/ gn /m/ mb /s/ c, ce, sc /zh/ s /sh/ ti, ci, ssi

Common exception words: of, to, the, into, are, do, were, one, our, their, floors, water, whole

Curriculum links: Science: Everyday materials; Design and technology: Evaluate

National Curriculum learning objectives: Reading/word reading: apply phonic knowledge and skills as the route to decode words, read accurately by blending sounds in unfamiliar words containing GPCs that have been taught, read common exception words, noting unusual correspondences between spelling and sound and where these occur in the word, read other words of more than one syllable that contain taught GPCs; Reading/comprehension: develop pleasure in reading, motivation to read, vocabulary and understanding by discussing word meanings

Developing fluency

- Your child may enjoy hearing you read the book.
- Take turns to read a page of the main text, encouraging your child to read any captions, labels, and **Fascinating fact** boxes too. If they stumble on exception words, suggest they reread the sentence.

Phonic practice

- Challenge your child to identify the different sounds made by the same spellings in the following words:

  gn: designed, signals   mb: climb, number   wh: whole, what
- Can they read and correctly sound out these words, noting the different sounds made by the last letter "c" in each?

  electric   electrician   electricity

Extending vocabulary

- Discuss the meaning of the adjective **renewable** on page 4. (*able to be renewed/resupplied*) Why is wind **renewable** but not coal? (*there is an endless supply of wind, but coal is limited*)
- Focus on the -able ending. Can they add -able to these words to make adjectives? Afterwards, discuss the meaning of each.

  break   move   afford   comfort